Krensky, Stephen.

The Constitution.

$34.21

DATE			

The CONSTITUTION

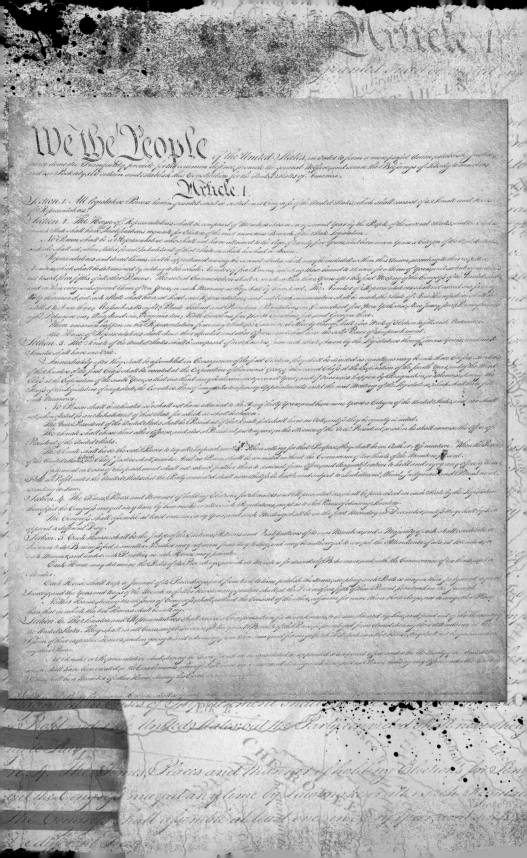

documents of
DEMOCRACY

The CONSTITUTION

by stephen krensky

MARSHALL CAVENDISH BENCHMARK
NEW YORK

With thanks to Catherine McGlone,
a lawyer with a special interest in constitutional law and American history,
for her legal eagle eye in perusing the manuscript

Other Marshall Cavendish Offices:
Marshall Cavendish International (Asia) Private Limited, 1 New Industrial Road, Singapore 536196 •
Marshall Cavendish International (Thailand) Co Ltd. 253 Asoke, 12th Flr, Sukhumvit 21 Road,
Klongtoey Nua, Wattana, Bangkok 10110, Thailand • Marshall Cavendish (Malaysia) Sdn Bhd, Times
Subang, Lot 46, Subang Hi-Tech Industrial Park, Batu Tiga, 40000 Shah Alam, Selangor Darul
Ehsan, Malaysia

Marshall Cavendish is a trademark of Times Publishing Limited
All websites were available and accurate when this book was sent to press.

LIBRARY OF CONGRESS CATALOGING-IN-PUBLICATION DATA
Krensky, Stephen. The Constitution / Stephen Krensky. p. cm. – (Documents of democracy Summary:
"An analysis of the U.S. Constitution, with information on how it was created and its impact on the
United States and the world"–Provided by publisher. Includes bibliographical references and index.
ISBN 978-0-7614-4917-1 – ISBN 978-1-60870-673-0 (ebook) 1. United States. Constitution–Juvenile
literature. 2. United States–Politics and government–1775-1783–Juvenile literature. 3. United States–
Politics and government–1783-1789–Juvenile literature. 4. Constitutional history–United States–
Juvenile literature. I. Title. E303.K74 2012 342.7302'9--dc22 2010040634

Editor: Joyce Stanton   Art Director: Anahid Hamparian
Publisher: Michelle Bisson   Series Designer: Michael Nelson

Photo research by Linda Sykes Picture Research, Inc., Hilton Head, SC
The photographs in this book are used by permission and through the courtesy of:
©Sean Locke/iStockphoto: cover; Steve Gottlieb/photolibrary: 1; iStockphoto/Sascha Burkard: 2;
The Granger Collection: 6, 8, 17, 19, 20, 22, 27, 31, 33, 40, 46, 49, 58, 68, 70, 71; Museum of Fine
Arts, Boston, MA/Seth K. Sweetser Fund/The Bridgeman Art Library: 13; Tetra Images/Corbis: 36;
Bettmann/Corbis: 43, 64; Library of Congress: 67.

Printed in Malaysia (T)
135642

Half-title page: Signing the Constitution
Title page: The opening words of the Constitution

Contents

A Country in Doubt

The country was in trouble. That much was certain. Whatever disagreements there were about how the trouble had started or what might be the best way to get out of it, something was seriously wrong. The victorious glow that had accompanied the successful American Revolution had largely faded away. A few years had passed, and now the thirteen states were often jealous and suspicious of one another. The unanswered question they shared was whether they should endow a national government with real power over them all—or continue individually to pretty much do as they pleased.

Above: **Independence Hall, as it looked in 1776**

Resolving this issue would not be easy. The fifty-five delegates from twelve states who came together in May 1787 knew that. (Only Rhode Island was missing. Its leaders were so opposed to even discussing the idea of a stronger union that they refused to take part.) Independence Hall in Philadelphia was the setting, a central location and a familiar meeting place for at least eight of the delegates, who had been among those gathered there eleven years earlier to create the Declaration of Independence.

For several weeks, the various sides debated the issues but made little headway. On June 26, Judge Oliver Ellsworth of Connecticut spoke for many when he said, "If you ask the States what is reasonable, they will comply. But if you ask of them more than is necessary to form a good government, they will grant you nothing."

James Madison, a delegate from Virginia and a man who had closely studied the options before them, shared this view. "That great powers are to be given, there is no doubt; and that those powers may be abused is equally true," he reminded the assembly. And yet Madison was not deterred by the enormity of the political task at hand. Nor was he interested in any makeshift or temporary solution that would have to be revisited in a few years. "The government we mean to erect," he declared, "is intended to last for ages."

The British surrender to General Washington at Yorktown, Virginia, 1781. Victory was won, but could the young republic survive?

Chapter One

A "Firm League of Friendship"

THE SUCCESS OF THE AMERICAN Revolution came as something of a surprise to all concerned. On the British side, there was shock and dismay. How could a ragtag group of colonies have managed to defeat the greatest country in the world? The whole thing was a nightmare—and an embarrassing one to boot. Still, it had truly happened, there was no denying that. The loss had shaken the British Empire—but even shaken, it was hardly in ruins. Canada remained firmly under its control as did many Caribbean islands and major outposts in distant India and Australia.

And besides, who was to say how permanent the loss of the American colonies might be? True, they had won their freedom, but who knew if they would be able to hold on to it? Already, the states were bickering among themselves like spoiled children. If the British patiently waited on the sidelines, perhaps the colonial alliance might fall apart and one or more of the colonies might be reclaimed.

For the brand-new Americans, there was a different kind of shock to absorb. Many of the rebellious patriots, while firmly believing in their cause, had never imagined they would be permanently separated from their mother country. They had fully expected Great Britain to realize its mistake early on in the fighting. A series of negotiations would follow and lead in due time to appropriate concessions. After the diplomatic dust had settled, the colonies surely would return to British rule.

But this scenario had not come to pass. Great Britain had remained firmly against reconciliation until it was too late and the war had been lost. So here stood the colonies, with peace officially settled by the Treaty of Paris in 1783 but without any definite idea of what should come next.

THE FIRST UNION

Not that the country was totally unprepared. Congress had done more than simply supervise the war following the Declaration of Independence in 1776. In fact, some centralizing of colonial control had taken place at the same time the Declaration was being written. On June 11 of that year, the Second Continental Congress appointed a committee to create what would come to be called the Articles of Confederation. These Articles, it was hoped, might someday govern a new nation. At that time, of course, the Revolution had yet to be won, and so creating the Articles was not exactly a priority.

It was important, however, to look ahead. The goal of the congressional committee was to try to balance the need for an effective central government against the independence each state desired. One of the issues discussed, for example, was how to calculate what each state would pay to the federal government in taxes. At first, it was proposed that each state's tax obligation would be based on its population. This might have seemed like a reasonable proposition, but the problem immediately arose as to whether slaves should be counted as part of a state's population. Since the slave-owning states did not consider slaves to be "people"—and since the additional numbers would increase their federal taxes—they thought slaves should not be counted. Naturally, those who were opposed to slavery thought the opposite.

There were other large issues as well. Should the states or Congress regulate relations with the various Indian tribes? And who should settle the disagreements surrounding some of the controversial state boundaries?

It took nearly a year and a half for the Articles to be ironed out. They were finally ready for signing in November 1777. Being ready was an important step, but it meant nothing by itself. Everyone understood that the Articles would go into effect only after every state had signed them. And not every state was in a hurry to do so. Nine states had ratified them by the following July, but four still had objections to be resolved. Not until Maryland finally signed off on March 1, 1781, did the Articles become law. A little more than seven months later, the British general Lord Cornwallis surrendered at Yorktown.

Not everyone thought that enacting the Articles represented a political victory. In commenting upon them, John Adams made this prediction on the floor of Congress: "This business, Sir, that has taken up so much of our time seems to be finished. But, Sir, I now, upon this floor, venture to predict that before ten years, this confederation, like a rope of sand, will be found inadequate to the purpose, and its dissolution will take place."

Adams's comment may have been prophetic, but the Articles themselves had modest goals. They were not formed to create a new country. They were actually designed to create something closer to a club—a club that all thirteen states had pledged to join. The club had rules and regulations, and maintaining them would be based on the willingness of all the members to participate in its activities and cooperate with

> "Sir, I now, upon this floor, venture to predict that before ten years, this confederation, like a rope of sand, will be found inadequate to the purpose, and its dissolution will take place."
>
> —John Adams, on the Articles of Confederation

John Adams in a formal portrait by the famous American artist John Singleton Copley

one another. The states were entering into what the Articles called a "firm league of friendship."

Under the Articles, every state could send between two and seven delegates, or representatives, to Congress. However, each state would only get one collective vote in any proceeding, regardless of its size or population or how many of its delegates were present. Each state was also left to itself to decide how much, if anything, to pay its delegates. A state could recall or substitute one delegate for another at any time it wished. And in order for Congress to undertake business, a minimum of seven out of the thirteen states, with at least two delegates each, had to be present. When this number was not in attendance, Congress could not meet.

Nine states had to be in agreement to pass legislation. This meant that it would take only five states to hold up any law from being passed. And since small states had the same voting power as large ones, the power to block laws could be held by a small fraction of the country as a whole. (For example, the Treaty of Paris remained unratified between November 26, 1783, and January 14, 1784, because Congress could not gather the nine state delegations necessary to vote for it.) States were also required to contribute money to a common defense, but each state could determine for itself how such money was to be raised.

However imperfect the Articles were, they represented a measure of progress toward an overall union, since they created a formal bond between the thirteen states. It was fortunate, too, that the Articles had been signed before the war ended. The states had made many compromises in order to come up with an agreement. Had there been no agreement in place before the victory at Yorktown, perhaps the states would have been unable to agree on any union at all.

LIFE UNDER THE ARTICLES

The problems with the Articles of Confederation appeared long before the war ended. At different junctures, Congress would issue a request for money or materials—and the states were supposed to respond to these requests. But no one was empowered to make them comply. So sometimes they did, and sometimes they didn't. Once the war was over, the states were even more disposed to ignore or be lazy about their national obligations because the immediate pressure of the war had been removed. This was true even though the war had left considerable debt for everyone to share.

One such obligation was army pay. In 1783, soldiers in the Continental army were being released from service. The soldiers were eager to return home, but they were just as eager to receive their pay before they left. They were reluctant to disperse for fear of never being paid at all. The army, which was camped at Newburgh, New York, was on the verge of mutiny.

There was talk that perhaps the only way Congress would understand the soldiers' plight was at the point of a bayonet. In fact, Congress understood the problem perfectly. It just had no money to pay the soldiers what they were owed.

At this crucial moment, General George Washington appeared. He wished to speak to his troops, and they put aside their anger to hear what he had to say. Standing before them, Washington began by putting on his reading glasses. "Gentlemen," he said, "you will permit me to put on my spectacles, for, I have grown not only gray, but almost blind, in the service of my country." He then asked them to be patient a while longer, and such was the men's regard for their beloved general that they agreed. And this was not the only such incident. A few months later, Congress hastily left Philadelphia for Princeton, New Jersey, because of the delegates' fear of being attacked by unpaid Pennsylvania troops (a fear that fortunately went unrealized).

The success of the Articles hinged upon the states' meeting their obligations. They were supposed to send money to support the national government. They were

> *"Gentlemen, you will permit me to put on my spectacles, for, I have grown not only gray, but almost blind, in the service of my country."*
> —George Washington

supposed to send troops to defend the country as a whole. And they were supposed to allow Congress to regulate commerce that crossed state lines. But being supposed to do something and actually doing it were not the same thing.

Another problem with the Articles was that all national authority rested in the one-house Congress. There was no independent executive branch or judiciary to make decisions and oversee the country in an ongoing way. Everything had to be run through Congress. The Articles' greatest weakness, however, was that they provided no direct connection between the national government and the people. All communication and laws were issued through the states. The national government was more of an appendage to the states, an arm or a leg, rather than the brain running the whole operation.

Still, some advances were made under the Articles of Confederation, notably in the area of land management. States claiming territories to the west of their borders gave up their claims to Congress. (Many of these states had claims stretching all the way to the Mississippi River.) This consolidation enabled Congress to oversee and administer the settling of those lands in an orderly fashion, notably in the Northwest Ordinance of 1787 (which included the future states of Ohio, Indiana, Illinois, Michigan, Wisconsin, and Minnesota).

By 1785, it was very clear that a change in the structure of government was needed. Although the former colonies had been united in spirit, especially during the Revolution, they were not so bound in other ways. Travel was difficult, with few roads, fewer bridges, and only occasional inns and public houses to safely spend the night. Only five cities had more than 10,000 residents, with New York at the top (33,000), followed by Philadelphia (28,500), Boston (18,000), Charleston (16,000), and Baltimore (13,500). The overall population of the United States was well over 3 million, so

New York City, 1797

people were clearly spread out. Given this dispersion, it was a stretch to think everyone could find common ground. There were divisions, too, between North and South, city and country, rich and poor, educated and uneducated, tradesmen and intellectuals, freemen and slaves. And some people, more than would publicly admit it, had been reluctant followers of the Revolution and still felt sentimental and intellectual ties to Great Britain.

So what should the leaders of the new nation do? Wisdom dictated that they take their time, and they did. Nothing dramatic happened at first, as the states adjusted to their new freedom. But in March 1785, delegates from Virginia and Maryland met to resolve some disagreements concerning boundaries and commerce. The success of this meeting prompted the two states to call for a wider convention in which all the states could address concerns about interstate commerce.

This gathering, called the Annapolis Convention, met in Annapolis, Maryland, in September 1786. Five states—New York, New Jersey, Pennsylvania, Delaware, and Virginia—discussed commercial issues of mutual interest. (The other states were invited, but chose not to send representatives.) Among the men meeting in Annapolis were James Madison of Virginia and Alexander Hamilton of New York, both of whom supported the idea of a stronger national

Alexander Hamilton, one of George Washington's most trusted advisers, became the first secretary of the treasury in 1789.

government. Neither of them, though, expected any real concrete advances to come out of the gathering. How could it succeed when representatives of only five states were present? What they hoped for was that one thing would lead to another. And they got their wish. A report of the meeting was sent to Congress, which then decided that convening all the states for the purpose of revising the Articles of Confederation was a good idea.

A further impetus for reform came from a violent uprising. Shays' Rebellion took place in western Massachusetts from August 1786 to February 1787. Local farmers and other small landowners were angry about losing their property because of their inability to pay taxes and other debts. They had asked the state legislature for relief, but had been rebuffed. Eventually, they gathered as a military force under the leadership of Daniel Shays, a Revolutionary War veteran. Although federal troops quickly defeated them, their uprising disturbed many people, coming as it did on the heels of the Revolution. And was sending soldiers to battle farmers who had legitimate grievances really the best way to settle a dispute? The incident made people question whether life was any better now than it had been under Great Britain. It also revealed the need for national leadership to resolve disputes that the individual states seemed unable to manage for themselves.

And so fifty-five delegates arrived in Philadelphia in May 1787 to see what they could accomplish. Overall, the delegates' ages were spread evenly along the spectrum. Twenty-five of them were fifty or older. Twenty-one were less than forty. At eighty-one, Benjamin Franklin of Pennsylvania was the oldest delegate. At twenty-six, Jonathan Dayton of New Jersey was the youngest. A significant number were lawyers or had studied the law, and among the rest were planters, doctors, ministers, and professors. Very quickly, a majority of the delegates decided that revising the Articles would not solve their problems. Instead, they would need to create a new plan of government: a constitution.

In an effort to achieve justice, Daniel Shays' rebels take control of a courthouse in western Massachusetts.

When one of his colonels suggested that he use the army to make himself king, Washington refused.

Chapter Two

The Constitution Takes Shape

OF THE EARLY PROGRESS AT THE Constitutional Convention, the most important accomplishment was getting George Washington, the hero of the Revolution, to come out of retirement to be its president. Washington had no equal among the Founding Fathers when it came to engendering trust. His reputation for honesty and integrity was respected by all, no small achievement in a group where someone was always suspecting someone else of trying to gain some political advantage.

Although Washington presided over the debates, he rarely spoke in the more public gatherings. But his presence was felt and his advice sought among the committees and in more private meetings. There was also a sense among the delegates (if not shared by Washington himself) that his involvement in any new government would be an absolute necessity for it to have a real chance to succeed.

Right from the beginning, there was a debate about what form this new government should take. The countries of Europe offered examples of both highly centralized states, such as England and France, and loosely knit confederations in the mold of the Italian and German states. Which model should the Americans follow? Should the states largely maintain their independence, sharing only a common need for security and commerce? Or should a truly united country be created, one in which the states were bound together under a strong central government? This was the key question the delegates would debate.

Looking to European models was tricky because the America of 1787 did not much resemble them. Compared to the rigid and layered European aristocracies, America was free and flexible. Admittedly, there were some wealthy individuals at the top of society, even if they weren't aristocrats. Still, a free newcomer without resources could land in the United States from abroad and make his fortune if he was lucky and capable enough. There were vast lands unspoken for and equally large natural resources available. In the European nations, there were no such opportunities for the peasants or underclass to exploit.

Then too, many of the former colonies had already created constitutions enabling their transition into states. Having done that, these same states valued their new individual powers and were reluctant to give them up, even in the interest of a promising national government. For some Americans, the concept of a faraway national government on the same side of the Atlantic was not much different from that of a colonial master overseas.

On the other hand, most of the delegates shared a common British heritage and were united in their regard for the British justice system. Great Britain had a long history of legal precedents that in some measure limited the power of the monarch and supported basic human rights. Perhaps the oldest document to influence the delegates was the Magna Carta of 1215. This agreement spelled out the first legal separation of powers between a monarch and his nobles. It limited royal power, establishing the premise that even the king had to obey the law. There were other documents as well. The Petition of Right from 1628 was the work of a frustrated British Parliament that felt King Charles I was abusing his power. The petition reminded him that, among other things, he could not make arbitrary arrests or create taxes without Parliament's consent. The Habeas Corpus Act of 1679 was a reminder that a person under arrest could not be unlawfully detained but rather had to be brought before a court of law in a timely fashion. In addition, the English Bill of Rights of 1689 listed a citizen's basic rights, which included freedom of speech and freedom from cruel and unusual punishment.

The delegates were also influenced by some of the great thinkers of the age. The book that affected them most was Montesquieu's *Spirit of Laws*, published in 1748. The French philosopher Montesquieu favored dividing government into three separate and independent branches—executive, legislative, and judicial. He believed that with the power of each branch balancing the others, the threat of tyranny could be avoided. Many of his ideas echoed the works of John Locke, an English philosopher writing about sixty years earlier. Locke had written at length to justify the existence of governments in the first place and to explain how they evolved from nature.

The delegates were united in another sense as well. They were highly motivated to build a strong new nation based on sound, workable principles. They had no doubt that many European powers, including former allies such as France and Spain, were hoping that their grand experiment in republicanism would fail. The delegates were also quite aware that other nations were laughing at them. Here they had managed to wrest their independence from Great Britain—and now they spent a lot of time squabbling among themselves. For a country forged in fiery speeches about independence and the rights of all men, it was hard not to be at least a little embarrassed about that.

Another point of agreement was the delegates' attitude toward church and state. Most wanted these

A POLITICALLY MINDED PHILOSOPHER

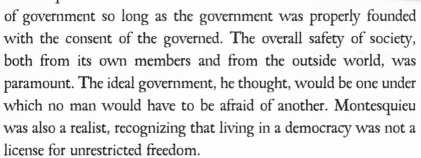

Charles-Louis de Secondat, baron de La Brède et de Montesquieu, lived from 1689 to 1755. An independently wealthy French aristocrat, Montesquieu was a firm believer in the value of government so long as the government was properly founded with the consent of the governed. The overall safety of society, both from its own members and from the outside world, was paramount. The ideal government, he thought, would be one under which no man would have to be afraid of another. Montesquieu was also a realist, recognizing that living in a democracy was not a license for unrestricted freedom.

Montesquieu had great faith in the collective wisdom of a people to choose good leaders. He also believed that in democracies the citizenry should be the only ones empowered to create laws. He advocated as well the idea of a separation of powers: "When the legislative and executive powers are united in the same person, or in the same body of magistrates, there can be no liberty; because apprehensions may arise, lest the same monarch or senate should enact tyrannical laws, to execute them in a tyrannical manner."

The writings of Montesquieu strongly influenced James Madison, who saw in them a worthy blueprint for political architecture. A government based on these ideas would be well anchored in the present and yet elastic enough to respond to unforeseen changes or crises in the future.

Above: The baron de Montesquieu in a painting by an unknown artist

institutions kept apart. The Puritans of Massachusetts and the Quakers of Pennsylvania might have had a large hand in the settling of their respective domains, but by this time their influence had receded. National leaders such as George Washington, Thomas Jefferson, Alexander Hamilton, and Benjamin Franklin shared the idea that religion was a personal matter that had no place in government. They might all acknowledge the existence of a Supreme Being, but they also believed that he had more important things to do than take an active role in their earthly affairs.

GETTING DOWN TO BUSINESS

While the delegates had to struggle to find a balance between the power of the central government and the rights of the individual states, they did firmly share one goal: They all wanted the new government to be strong enough to rule the nation. At the same time, they wanted it to respect the liberties of the states and the human rights of the citizens.

Compromise was the answer.

Delegates from the large states, for example, disagreed with those from the small states about representation in the national legislature. While it was not surprising that the smaller states would worry about being overwhelmed by the larger ones, it also made sense that larger populations deserved more representation than smaller ones. The large states favored the Virginia Plan, proposed by Edmund Randolph of Virginia. Under this plan, a state's population would determine the number of representatives it could send to the legislature. The small states supported the New Jersey Plan, proposed by William Paterson, under which every state would have an equal number of representatives. To bring the two sides together, the Connecticut delegates suggested a compromise: a two-house legislature in which representation in the lower house would be based on population while representation in the upper house would be equal for each state, regardless of its size or population. (Caught in the middle of this issue was how to count the slaves living in each state. They were considered property on the one hand but also part of the general population on the other. A middle ground was found by deciding that slaves would be recorded at a reduced rate: three would be counted for every five who lived in a given location.)

The bicameral, or two-house, legislature was an important principle to emerge from the debates at the Constitutional Convention. Another was the concept of a balanced national government in which authority would be divided among three separate branches—the executive, the legislative, and the judicial. Each branch would be independent of the others, and so each branch could use its powers if necessary to check, or curb, the actions of the other two.

MORE BALANCING ACTS

To try to keep the power of the federal government in line with the rights of the states and the people, the delegates expressly defined certain of its powers. The federal government had the right to collect taxes, declare war, and regulate trade. It was also given "implied" powers, those reasonably suggested by the Constitution, which would enable the federal government to respond to the nation's changing needs over time.

However, some powers were not given to the federal government. These "reserved" powers were delegated to the people or to the states instead. The states could pass laws concerning marriage, divorce, and public education. Powers reserved for the people included the right to own property and to be tried by a jury if accused of a crime.

The Supreme Court was given the final authority to protect the Constitution against incursions from the other branches or the states. Most importantly, it was empowered to set aside any law that in its judgment conflicted with any part of the constitutional mandates.

A CONSENSUS IS REACHED

By July 24, about two months after the delegates had convened, they had reached considerable agreement. A Committee of Detail was then created, consisting of Edmund Randolph of Virginia, Nathaniel Gorman of Massachusetts, John Rutledge of South Carolina, Oliver Ellsworth of Connecticut, and James Wilson of Pennsylvania. On August 6, they reported back with a draft that contained a preamble and twenty-three articles, including fifty-seven sections. This draft was debated for another month. On September 8, the Committee of Style and Arrangement was appointed to do a revision. Its members included Alexander Hamilton of New York, James Madison of Virginia, Gouverneur Morris of Pennsylvania, William Johnson of Connecticut,

George Washington's copy of the August 6 draft, with the corrections he made

"It . . . astonishes me, sir, to find this system approaching so near to perfection as it does."

—Benjamin Franklin, on the Constitution

and Rufus King of Massachusetts. The final literary touches were credited to Morris, both by himself and later by Madison. On September 17, 1787, the document was finished.

On August 31, the delegates had voted that ratification by nine states would be enough to establish the Constitution in those states. This was a critically important decision since it meant that if nine states were willing to go ahead as a country, they would do that, whether the remaining states chose to join them or not.

Benjamin Franklin wrote a final speech marking the completion of the Constitution. Unfortunately he was too ill to present his speech to the convention in person, so he asked his friend James Wilson to read it aloud to the other delegates. It included the following observation:

When you assemble a number of men, to have the advantage of their joint wisdom, you inevitably assemble with those men all their prejudices, their passions, their errors of opinion, their local interests, and their selfish views. From such an assembly, can a perfect production be expected? It therefore astonishes me, sir, to find this system approaching so near to perfection as it does.

WHO WROTE THE CONSTITUTION?

Unlike the Declaration of Independence, which was widely attributed to Thomas Jefferson, the Constitution was not seen as the work of any one man. Various delegates to the Constitutional Convention contributed to the document's creation. One who did not take an active part was Benjamin Franklin, who was weakened by age and illness. And two of the most prominent leaders of the period, John Adams and Thomas Jefferson, were not present for equally good reasons: Jefferson was the ambassador to France and Adams the ambassador to Great Britain, and both of them were abroad at their posts during this period.

James Madison is usually cited as the man who contributed the most to the document. Credit is given to him for his profound understanding of the issues involved, not because of his writing skills. Much of the Constitution was singularly plain in its presentation. There were no literary flourishes in the various articles, an omission that reflected the mind of the no-nonsense Madison.

He was a Virginian, born in 1751. He grew up at Montpelier, a plantation not far from Thomas Jefferson's home at Monticello. A member of the Virginia House of Delegates during the Revolution, he also served in Congress from 1780 to 1783. Later, Madison was President Jefferson's secretary of state and was the fourth president himself from 1808 to 1816.

Above: **James Madison**

The document was then given to Congress to pass on to the states. There was no assurance at this point, however, that the Constitution would become the law of the land. Only forty-two of the original fifty-five delegates were still present when the deliberations ended, and three of them refused to sign the final version. While George Washington and Benjamin Franklin were strongly supportive (which meant a great deal), such local patriots as Patrick Henry of Virginia, Governor George Clinton of New York, and Governor John Hancock of Massachusetts were either definitely opposed or mildly skeptical.

Some critics thought the Constitution gave Congress too many powers and that the proposed federal government was too strong. Others thought the Senate was too aristocratic. There were also objections that a bill of rights had not been included. Supporters of the Constitution, who became known as the Federalists, rallied to urge its ratification. A series of newsletters appeared, written under the name of a certain "Publius." Called the Federalist Papers, they were actually the work of Alexander Hamilton, James Madison, and John Jay of New York. Opponents of ratification were called Anti-Federalists. Eventually, the two groups would develop into the nation's first political parties.

The first state to approve the Constitution was Delaware, on December 7, 1787. Pennsylvania was added on the 12th and New Jersey on the 18th. Massachusetts ratified by a close vote on February 6, 1788. When New Hampshire voted to ratify on June 21, 1788, it was the ninth state to do so, putting the Constitution into effect. This victory for the Federalists felt complete when the important states of Virginia and New York came aboard shortly afterward. Only North Carolina and Rhode Island were still undecided. Faced with the possibility of being treated as foreign nations surrounded by a single United States, they eventually came around—North Carolina in November 1789 and Rhode Island on May 29, 1790.

The fledgling republic was ready to test its wings. It remained to be seen, though, how far it would get off the ground. However the future might turn out, James Madison expressed himself with conviction when he described the events of the moment: "There never was an assembly of men, charged with a great and arduous trust, who were more pure in their motives, or more exclusively or anxiously devoted to the object committed to them, than were the members of the Federal Convention of 1787."

We the People of the United

insure domestic Tranquility, provide for the common defense, promote the
and our Posterity, do ordain and establish this Constitution for the Unit

Article 1

So far, the U.S. Constitution has stood
the test of time.

Chapter Three

Becoming *the* United States

AT ITS HEART, THE CONSTITUTION HAD a very different intent from, say, the Declaration of Independence. The Declaration was a call to arms. It was meant to provoke and inspire. It was meant to set forth the philosophical ideas that would justify a revolt against generations of tradition. That it succeeded in these goals was a testament both to the ideas it contained and to the words that expressed them.

The purpose of the Constitution was something else. The war was over. But with the arrival of peace, complications had set in. What course was best for the barely united states? Though a lot of people were pleased to see the Constitution take effect, that didn't mean they weren't worried about it. After all, what if the new national government turned out to be as bad as the British tyranny the country had just defeated? Then too, regional interests and jealousies threatened to undo the victory that had so dearly been won.

To satisfy these various factions, a successful document had to be clear and dry, almost detached in its appeal to reason. Its words needed to subdue frayed tempers and soothe nervous dispositions. Building a new government almost from scratch was not a task for the fainthearted, but it was also not a time for bombast and exaggeration to lead the way. A calm and rational approach was required.

THE PREAMBLE

The first seven words of the Constitution are "We the People of the United States." These seven words signified an announcement in themselves. Never before had the "people" been taken together in a national sense, rising above local or regional loyalties. The Articles of Confederation had not endorsed or allowed anything like that. The states had reigned supreme under the Articles. That would be true no longer.

The rest of the preamble continues: "in Order to form a more perfect Union, establish Justice, insure domestic Tranquility, provide for the common defence, promote the general Welfare, and secure the Blessings of Liberty to ourselves and our Posterity, do ordain and establish this Constitution for the United States of America." While the sentiments expressed here echoed those of the Declaration of Independence, the document that followed created a framework for government more ambitious than anything the leaders of the new nation had originally imagined. Each of the seven articles of the Constitution addressed a specific area of the law and government while at the same time leaving room for interpretation and allowing for adjustments to be made over time.

ARTICLE I: THE LEGISLATIVE BRANCH

Article I began by defining the legislative part of the national government: "All legislative Powers herein granted shall be vested in a Congress of the United States, which shall consist of a Senate and House of Representatives." Neither of these two branches could enact a law by itself. (In this way, they would deliberately need to act together to get anything accomplished.) Significantly, no other branch of the government, executive or judicial, was authorized to create laws at all.

In the House of Representatives, members would be elected every two years. The short term was meant to ensure that the representatives would remain attentive to their constituents. Each representative would have to be at least twenty-five years old and to have been an American citizen for at least seven years. (As a short-term solution to a potentially awkward legality, anyone born in a territory that subsequently became a state would automatically become a

"All legislative Powers herein granted shall be vested in a Congress of the United States, which shall consist of a Senate and House of Representatives."

—Article I, Section 1

The House of Representatives in the early 1800s

citizen.) A representative would also have to live in the state his district was part of, but not necessarily in the district itself. (Representatives have traditionally lived in their districts, though, in order to meet local voters and gain their support.)

The number of representatives in the House would be based on the general population of each state. Each state would have at least one representative, and there would be no more than one for every 30,000 persons. (In 1929, Congress fixed the total number of representatives at 435.) Importantly, the population of a state would be determined "by adding to the whole Number of free Persons"—with "free Persons" including those bound to service for a term of years and Indians who paid taxes—"three fifths of all other Persons." Those "other Persons" meant the slaves. A census would be held every ten years to update the population totals. All bills for raising revenue would originate in the House.

In the Senate, two senators would be chosen from each state. They would be elected to serve for six years. In contrast to the terms of the representatives, their longer terms were intended to provide an element of political stability. As a further check against the whims of public sentiment, senators would not be elected directly by the general population. Instead, they would be elected by their state legislatures. (In 1913, the Seventeenth Amendment changed this procedure, mandating direct election of senators by the public.)

A senator would have to be thirty years old, a citizen for at least nine years, and live in the state from which he was elected. Although the first group of senators would be elected simultaneously, they would then be divided into three groups. One group would run for reelection in two years and a second group in four. (After that, their six-year terms would commence.) The third group would have a six-year term from the start. Therefore, once this schedule was implemented, only one-third of the Senate would ever come up for election at a time (as opposed to the House of Representatives, whose members would all come up for election every two years).

Additionally, the vice president would be the president of the Senate, but his presence would be ceremonial except in those cases where a vote resulted in a tie. At such times, the vice president would cast a vote to support one side or the other.

Although the delegates to the Constitutional Convention foresaw the importance of Congress in the coming years, they were less sure of how much time congressional business would take. Therefore the Constitution directed that "Congress shall assemble at least once in every Year, and such Meeting shall be on the first Monday in December, unless they shall by Law appoint a different Day."

The delegates took very seriously the possibility of government officials abusing their power or acting inappropriately and therefore having to be removed from office. In such cases, either house could expel one of its members by a two-thirds vote.

The composition of Congress was described in considerable detail because it was to be given a great deal of exclusive power. Going forward, only Congress was empowered to declare war, raise and support an army and navy, and negotiate with foreign governments. Congress would punish crimes against the United States whether on land or sea. The only exception would be in the case of a state being suddenly attacked from abroad. In that instance, with time clearly being critical, a state could act to defend itself rather than wait for an authorization from Congress. The power of Congress was curbed, however, when it came to protecting an individual from unlawful imprisonment: Congress was forbidden to suspend the writ of habeas corpus except in cases of rebellion or invasion, when "the public Safety may require it."

HABEAS CORPUS

The words *habeas corpus* are Latin. They literally mean "you should have the body." In English and American law, *body* doesn't mean a corpse. It refers to the body of evidence necessary in order to detain a person. The right of habeas corpus is one of the cornerstones of freedom, for it protects an individual against unlawful imprisonment. The government must show a writ of habeas corpus—some sort of proof that a person should be detained—in a timely fashion or the accused may go free.

The right of habeas corpus began in England in the 1200s, when the king and his nobles were jockeying for power. Its foundations go back to the Magna Carta, written in 1215. From that document, it was established that the liberty of a king's subjects could not be restrained without an adequate reason.

The procedure for issuing the writs was established in 1679, in the Habeas Corpus Act. Supporters of the act were moved by the fear that when and if the Catholic James Stuart took the throne (which he did in 1685, after the death of his brother Charles II), he might imprison many of his perceived Protestant enemies without just cause.

During the course of its history, the right of habeas corpus was not always honored in England, especially in times of war. In spite of that, by the time of the American Revolution, it was widely considered a hallmark of enlightened political thinking. As such, it received special mention in the Constitution.

Above: King John I of England, looking none too happy in this modern illustration, signs the Magna Carta.

In economic matters, Congress was exclusively given the power to impose and collect taxes and other levies, coin money, and set a standard for weights and measures. In terms of commerce, the states would all be considered one entity, with no taxes or duties imposed on one state when shipping goods to another. Congress would also be in charge of maintaining post roads and running the post office. And only Congress could consent to economic agreements with other countries, whether regarding treaties, loans, bills of credit, taxes on imports, or inspections of foreign goods. "To promote the Progress of Science and useful Arts," Congress would secure copyright protection to ensure the rights of authors and inventors.

The procedure for enacting laws was quite specific:

Every Bill which shall have passed the House of Representatives and the Senate, shall, before it become a Law, be presented to the President of the United States: If he approve he shall sign it, but if not he shall return it, with his Objections to that House in which it shall have originated, who shall enter the Objections at large on their Journal, and proceed to reconsider it. If after such Reconsideration two thirds of that House shall agree to pass the Bill, it shall be sent, together with the Objections, to the other House, by which it shall likewise be reconsidered, and if approved by two thirds of that House, it shall become a Law.

And just in case anyone had any doubt about the Constitution fostering an aristocracy, Article I stated definitively that "No Title of Nobility shall be granted by the United States." Additionally, no person in office could accept, without the consent of Congress, any gift from a representative of a foreign government.

The significance of Article I was both dramatic and far-reaching, addressing the thorny problem of balancing national versus individual state interests. Under its provisions, Congress, for example, was given a direct and independent ability to raise money for national needs (something the Articles of Confederation had deliberately omitted). Also, Article I empowered the federal government to act directly in the national interest in a wide variety of circumstances without first requiring any state-by-state approval.

ARTICLE II: THE EXECUTIVE BRANCH

Article II outlined the election and responsibilities of the president. The president was a single executive who would be advised by a council, the cabinet. Only a natural-born citizen (or a citizen of the United States at the time the Constitution was enacted) at least thirty-five years old could serve. Additionally, a candidate had to have been a resident of the United States for at least fourteen years.

And that was all. Anyone who met these requirements could in theory do the job—although the founders were presumably starting from the assumption that the president would be a white male. Even allowing for that significant filter, this was a dramatic change. Previous forms of government had drawn their leaders from well-established families in either the aristocracy or the military. But an American president didn't have to boast of an education or own land or have money in his pocket. He simply had to be a man others would put their faith in. Never before had a government been created that left so much room from which a leader could rise. Of course, if a president wasn't rich, the presidential salary of $25,000 a year would certainly help pay the bills. (The first president, George Washington, declined his salary, being a wealthy man already.)

The president's powers were to be considerable. Originally, the Senate wanted to call the chief executive His Highness the President of the United States of America and Protector of their Liberties. The House thought this sounded too much like the title of a king and proposed the much simpler President of the United States.

The president could not inherit his job, nor could he be appointed. He had to be elected, for a four-year term, and his position did not place him above the law. It was clearly stated that the "President, Vice President and all civil Officers of the United States, shall

George Washington lived in this Philadelphia town house while he was president.

be removed from Office on Impeachment for, and Conviction of, Treason, Bribery, or other high Crimes and Misdemeanors."

This was an important safeguard, since the president was made supreme commander of all military forces. Being in charge of the military, however, did not mean the president could order troops to do whatever he wanted. It was important that one leader had the power to act quickly and decisively in times of need, but even so, only Congress could officially declare war. If the president saw fit to deploy troops for battle, he would need congressional support. Similarly, the president, while in charge of making treaties with other nations, was required to get the "Advice and Consent" of the Senate. Two-thirds of the senators would need to support the president's position for a treaty to take effect.

As chief executive, the president could veto congressional legislation, a veto that only a two-thirds vote of Congress could override, which normally would be difficult to attain. He was empowered to nominate and, again with the advice and consent of the Senate, to appoint ambassadors, public ministers, and judges of the Supreme Court. In all, it was an extremely powerful job. And had it not been for the fact that everyone thought George Washington—a person universally trusted—would be the first man to hold the office, the presidency might have been defined more narrowly. Not only was it taken for granted that Washington would be a great and honorable president, but it was also assumed that he would set such a strong example that later presidents would follow his lead.

ARTICLE III: THE JUDICIAL BRANCH

"The judicial Power of the United States shall be vested in one supreme Court, and in such inferior Courts as the Congress may from time to time ordain and establish."

Under the Articles of Confederation, there had been no absolute judicial authority governing the states. The Constitution would change that. The judicial branch created by the Constitution would be independent of

John Marshall, fourth chief justice of the Supreme Court, served for thirty-four years. He is credited with raising the judicial branch of the federal government to a level equal to that of the executive and legislative branches.

the legislative and executive branches—a condition not found in other governments. The hope was that an independent judiciary would be subject to as little political pressure as possible when making its judgments, a situation that would ensure the fairest rulings.

Article III established the Supreme Court as the final arbiter for legal decisions, recognizing that lower courts would also exist under its domain. Its judicial power would extend over all issues covered by the Constitution, whether between citizens or noncitizens, whether in one state or in a case that crossed state lines. (However, the Eleventh Amendment to the Constitution, which was ratified in 1795, limited the power of the federal judiciary in cases concerning foreign citizens or when an American citizen wished to sue a state other than the one he lived in.)

The Supreme Court would directly adjudicate in cases involving ambassadors from other countries or other foreign officials, since this was inevitably a national rather than a state matter. It would also rule in cases "in which a State shall be Party" so that state would not end up in the position of adjudicating on itself. Otherwise, the Supreme Court would act as a court of appeals should the ruling of a lower court be challenged. Article III also stipulated that careful steps would be taken to make sure federal courts and state courts did not oversee the same issues.

No preestablished requirements were enumerated for becoming a federal judge or Supreme Court justice. All such judges or justices, though, would have to be appointed by the president and confirmed by the Senate. Presumably, therefore, viable candidates would have sufficiently impressive credentials. These appointments would last for as long as the judges wished to hold them, which made it most imperative that a judge be qualified. Only a judge convicted of improper behavior could be removed against his will.

Article III also addressed criminal trials: all criminal trials, except those of impeachment, would be jury trials, and those trials would be held in the state in which the crime took place. This provision was meant to allay any fears that the national government would make off with local rights. If a crime was committed locally, then it would be ruled on locally as well.

The last section of Article III concerned the act of treason. It defined treason as making war directly against the United States or providing assistance to its enemies. Although this provision seemed straightforward enough, it actually represented a distinct change from English law. In Great Britain, treason could also be brought as a charge against counterfeiters and anyone having sexual relations with a member of the royal family (if those relations clouded the issue of royal succession). English law also allowed for tainting of descendants of a traitor (which might result in losing certain rights or living under a cloud of suspicion). The Constitution forbade any such punishment or penalty for a relative of a traitor simply because of the connection by blood.

ARTICLE IV: DEFINING THE ROLE OF THE STATES

Article IV was all about the states—establishing guidelines for governing the individual relationships among them and their collective relationship to the federal government. First, the article made it clear that the laws and records of each state had to be honored by the other states. Anyone, for example, who committed a crime in one state and fled to another, only to be captured there, would be returned to the state where the crime had been committed at that state's request.

The article defended a state's rights in other ways. On the territorial front, new states could not be made out of existing ones without the consent of the legislatures of the states affected by the change as well as the approval of Congress.

Article IV also stated that the federal government would guarantee to each state a republican form of government and provide military protection in case the state was invaded.

Much of the article was taken word for word from the earlier Articles of Confederation. It was important here to show that the Articles of Confederation were gone but not entirely forgotten. In this way, the delegates to the Constitutional Convention hoped to allay the fears of those who worried that states' rights would be subsumed under the power of the new federal government.

ARTICLE V: AMENDING THE CONSTITUTION

Article V outlined the procedure for making permanent changes to the Constitution in the form of amendments. The Founding Fathers were wise enough to realize that differing circumstances in the future might necessitate the altering of existing law. However, they also wanted to make it difficult to enact such changes, so that no mere fad or emotional surge, even in a time of crisis, would become the law of the land.

The article allowed for amendments this way: "The Congress, whenever two thirds of both Houses shall

"If in the opinion of the people . . . the Constitutional powers be in any particular wrong, let it be corrected by an amendment . . . , but let there be no change by usurpation; for though this, in one instance may be the instrument of good, it is the customary weapon by which free governments are destroyed."

—George Washington, from his Farewell Address, September 17, 1796

deem it necessary, shall propose Amendments to this Constitution, or, on the Application of the Legislatures of two thirds of the several States, shall call a Convention for proposing Amendments." At that point, three-quarters of the states would have to ratify the amendment before it became law.

There were, however, some clauses in the Constitution that could not be changed at all. One was the first clause in Section 9 of Article I, which stated that the importation of slaves could not be prohibited until 1808. At the time, there were about 650,000 slaves nationwide, 90 percent of whom lived in five states: Maryland, Virginia, North Carolina, South Carolina, and Georgia. If this clause had not been written into the Constitution (or had slavery simply been outlawed, as many at the convention wished to see happen), these five states probably would have voted against ratification. In that case, there very likely would have been no permanent union at all.

Making this clause exempt from amendment quieted the anxieties of the proslavery states, which feared that the federal government might simply abolish slavery or the importation of slaves after the Constitution was passed. So, in another compromise, the delegates agreed that no amendments to this clause would be allowed for a generation. Congress did indeed ban the importation of slaves in 1808.

Part of the first clause of Section 3 of Article I also could not be amended. It concerned the makeup of the Senate, in which each state elected two senators regardless of its size or population. Making this provision immune to change was meant to reassure the smaller states that their equal representation in the Senate would never be overturned or modified in the future. "No State," Article V provided, "without its Consent, shall be deprived of its equal Suffrage in the Senate."

ARTICLE VI: "THE SUPREME LAW OF THE LAND"

The Constitution and the laws emanating from it would now be the final authority for any dispute within the country or for governing any treaty outside it. Unlike the Articles of Confederation, the Constitution was creating a true national government. The document was to be "the supreme Law of the Land"—clear and forceful words to avoid any ambiguity. Historians, in fact, have called this section, known as the supremacy clause, the linchpin of the Constitution. Without it, the structure of the government might eventually have fallen apart.

To emphasize the importance of the Constitution, all elected representatives, whether at the national, state, or local level, would be bound by oath to support and uphold it. Again, this point underscored the Constitution's position as the basis of a national government. It was much more than merely an organizational tool for helping the states to get along with one another. Elected representatives would not be at liberty to do as they pleased—if what they pleased was different from what the Constitution allowed. And if state laws conflicted with national laws, the national laws would be supreme.

Article VI firmly established the United States of America as a single country, not the looser group of states it had been under the Articles of Confederation. However, the Articles of Confederation were not being repudiated in a legal sense; they were simply being replaced. Therefore, "All Debts contracted and Engagements entered into, before the Adoption of this Constitution, shall be as valid against the United States under this Constitution, as under the Confederation."

It was also noted here that "no religious Test shall ever be required as a Qualification" for holding federal office. Interestingly, this was mentioned almost casually—as though it wasn't a very big deal. But in fact the opposite was true. Putting into law that no religious affiliation was required or preferred in order to hold federal office was in many ways as revolutionary as anything else in the document. Even in religiously tolerant countries, there was inevitably one religion that held an edge, and to erase that edge here as a matter of law was very significant.

ARTICLE VII: LAYING THE RATIFICATION GROUNDWORK

Article VII explained that to put the Constitution into effect, the "Ratification of the Conventions of nine States, shall be sufficient." Nine was not a number picked by accident. From a total of thirteen states, nine represented a two-thirds majority. Two-thirds was considered a more significant proof of support than a simple majority (which would have been seven). Proponents argued that if nine states voted in favor of the Constitution, then opponents could hardly claim that they were barely outnumbered. Of course, since all the states were not equal in size or population, it was still important for the larger states to ratify, in order to give the new country a reasonable chance of survival. And the states that geographically lay in the middle—Virginia, Pennsylvania, and New York, for example—had an added importance. If any of them chose to stand apart, then the remaining United States would in some fashion be cut in two.

It was understood that once any nine states approved the Constitution, the document would become law in those nine states, no matter what the remaining states decided to do. Once the Constitution went into effect, any states that formally rejected ratification would then be treated like foreign countries. Rhode Island, for example, strongly resisted joining the other states in a national government. But if nine or more states signed up, pressure would build on Rhode Island to join. It was one thing to have the power to keep the Constitution from ever going into effect (as was true under the Articles of Confederation, when any one state could veto a proposal). It was something else to be surrounded by Constitution-abiding states, to be isolated from them in commerce and defense. So in the end, even reluctant Rhode Island came around, the last of the thirteen states to vote for ratification.

NO GOING BACK

Without question, the Constitution represented a significant change from the Articles of Confederation. Defenders of states' rights were quick to point out that the new national government was granted only those powers that it would be impractical for the states to administer themselves. This was true, but those powers were extensive and covered every aspect of the new nation's political and economic life. The Constitution was a bold and unprecedented experiment in government. Whether it would succeed or fail had yet to be seen, but its framers firmly believed it was their best chance for ensuring the survival of the new republic.

In a victory for the Federalists, particularly New York's Alexander Hamilton, crowds line lower Manhattan to celebrate the Constitution's ratification.

Chapter Four

A New Era Begins

WERE THE AMERICAN STATES TRULY in danger of going their separate ways had the Constitution not been written? There's no way of knowing for certain. In 1787, no conflict appeared bad enough to precipitate the instant dissolution of the Articles of Confederation. However, the signs of stress, unrest, and disagreement would never have gone away by themselves. Sooner or later, a crisis would have emerged. In addition, powerful empires like Great Britain and Spain (both of which wished for any alternative to one strong nation uniting the eastern coast of North America) could have eventually prompted the fragile pre-Constitution union to fall apart. The result might have been thirteen independent states or, more likely, two or more countries formed by several states banding together.

That this did not occur, of course, was the first ramification of the Constitution's adoption. It ushered in a

> *"Our new Constitution is now established and has an appearance that promises permanency; but in this world nothing can be said to be certain, except death and taxes."*
>
> *—Benjamin Franklin*

new era in American history, though there was nothing guaranteed about how long that era might last. As Benjamin Franklin wrote to a friend in France, "Our new Constitution is now established and has an appearance that promises permanency; but in this world nothing can be said to be certain, except death and taxes."

Even if the Constitution did not ensure anything permanent, it was a very big step in the right direction. Admittedly, though, it was far from perfect. In fact, it was so imperfect that the framers promptly proposed a set of amendments. There were ten of them, and they became law in December 1791 when, as the Constitution dictated, three-quarters of the states had ratified them.

THE BILL OF RIGHTS

The first ten amendments, known collectively as the Bill of Rights, were largely concerned with the protection of personal freedoms. They were introduced in response to criticism that the Constitution had established a framework of government without ensuring the proper personal liberties to go with it. They were considered so important that many state delegates had only agreed to ratify the Constitution with the understanding that Congress would immediately set to work on a group of amendments that would protect individual rights.

Among these rights were freedom of religion and speech, the right to peaceably assemble and to petition the government for a redress of grievances, the right to keep and bear arms, the right to a criminal trial by jury, and the right to legal counsel. Individuals would be protected against "cruel and unusual punishments." They could not be forced to quarter troops or to undergo unreasonable search and seizure. Perhaps most importantly, no person could be deprived of life, liberty, or property "without due process of law." In addition, the last of the ten amendments reassured people that the power of the federal government would be restrained. It stipulated that any rights not delegated to the federal government by the Constitution, or prohibited by the Constitution to the states, would remain the rights of the states or the people. (The Bill of Rights is discussed in greater detail in its own book in the DOCUMENTS OF DEMOCRACY series.)

Other amendments followed, though more slowly. The idea of peacefully introducing political change through amendments rather than through revolution or military force was a significant step in keeping the political fabric of the country from coming unraveled. As President Washington said in his Farewell Address on September 17, 1796:

If in the opinion of the people the distribution or modification of the Constitutional powers be in any particular wrong, let it be corrected by an amendment in the way which the Constitution designates, but let there be no change by usurpation; for though this, in one instance may be the instrument of good, it is the customary weapon by which free governments are destroyed.

SLAVERY FRONT AND CENTER

The largest challenge facing the Constitution, and by extension the continued existence of the United States itself, surrounded the issue of slavery. From the time of the Declaration of Independence, the problem loomed over all national discussions like a dark cloud that everyone wished would simply blow away on its own. But that wasn't going to happen.

The North framed the slavery debate in ethical and moral terms. The South relied on the concept of states' rights to justify the continued practice of slavery, maintaining that it was a question that every state should decide for itself. Southern states didn't want northern states bossing them around, whatever the issue might be. Of course, they also knew that slavery was so economically ingrained in their society that they couldn't survive without it. And since they liked their society the way it was, sanctioning slavery, even if it was morally wrong, was a price they were willing to pay.

But the tension between the two sides could not continue indefinitely. And it grew in intensity as more and more states joined the union. In the end, the issue came to a head in the Civil War. Following the Union victory, the Thirteenth Amendment, which banned slavery, was passed. The amendment, however, failed to correct many of the injustices African Americans faced. Several states found bureaucratic ways to keep the former slaves in their place. In some places, they were prevented from voting and enjoying other benefits of citizenship. Further amendments (notably the Fourteenth, Fifteenth, and Twenty-fourth) tried to address these problems. Even today, long after the abolition of slavery, prejudice and bigotry remain active forces—notwithstanding the 2008 election of the first African American president, Barack Obama.

Other amendments over the years have dealt with a variety of topics, from establishing a federal income tax, to changing the date of the presidential inauguration, to limiting the office of the president to two terms. The most far-reaching change beyond the elimination of slavery, though, was the Nineteenth Amendment, ratified in 1920, which gave women the right to vote.

THE CONSTITUTION AT RISK

While the Constitution's intent was to unite the country and protect individual liberties, its lofty goals have

ALMOST AN AMENDMENT

Thousands of amendments have been proposed to the Constitution since 1789. Of these, twenty-seven have actually been ratified, and they reflect changes in American attitudes and customs over the last two-hundred-plus years. While the most prominent among them have dealt with such historic issues as ending slavery or giving women the

Above: ERA supporters rally in New York City in 1980 to urge ratification of the controversial amendment.

right to vote, others have been less far-reaching. But whether large or small, any amendment to the Constitution undergoes the same process, requiring support from a large portion of the population.

Perhaps the most controversial amendment that received the necessary two-thirds vote from Congress (but never became law) was the Equal Rights Amendment (ERA). It read in part: "Equality of rights under the law shall not be denied or abridged by the United States or by any state on account of sex." The amendment was passed by Congress in 1972. However, there was much controversy about the unintended effects it might have on everyday life. Critics declared that existing amendments already guaranteed a woman's right to vote and every citizen's right to be treated equally.

The Equal Rights Amendment was unable to garner the necessary three-quarters support from the states and it expired without becoming law. In the years since, existing laws have continued to broaden their scope, addressing many of the issues the ERA raised.

not always been met. Abuses have arisen—sometimes under the guise of benefiting the people.

One early example of a constitutional challenge occurred in 1798, with the passage of the Alien and Sedition Acts. At the time, the United States was engaged in a military dispute with France. The bills' supporters, including President John Adams, maintained that the legislation was needed to protect the United States from verbal and written attacks. Under its provisions, for example, freedom of speech was not allowed if the speech criticized the government's actions. The bills' critics maintained that the proposed legislation clearly violated the constitutional right to freedom of speech. Its true purpose, they argued, was to shield the Federalists in power from being attacked for their actions. Two years later, a new president, Thomas Jefferson, took office. He pardoned anyone who had been arrested under the provisions of the Alien and Sedition Acts.

Wartime often had a way of pushing the Constitution aside for what was considered the greater good of the country as a whole. In 1861, President Abraham Lincoln took several steps that bypassed constitutional rule. He suspended the right of habeas corpus and had 13,000 people arrested who were suspected of being Confederate sympathizers. He also suspended civil law in certain western territories (beyond the Mississippi River) in order to maintain military control. Eighty years later, after the Japanese attack on Pearl Harbor in

Taking the pledge, 1942, at a public school in San Francisco. Shortly after this photo was shot, all of the Japanese American children in it were sent away to internment camps for the duration of the war.

Hawaii, 110,000 Japanese Americans, mostly in California, were arrested and interned out of a fear that they would assist in or support a Japanese invasion. The internment was not only unconstitutional (since there was no proof the Japanese Americans had done or intended to do anything disloyal), it was also racist, because no similar steps were taken to intern German Americans or Italian Americans, both of whose ancestral homelands were allied with the Japanese. (Forty-seven years later, in 1988, Congress passed legislation apologizing for the internment and paid financial compensation to the survivors and their families.)

CLASHING JURISDICTIONS

Although the Constitution tried to spell out the differences between federal and state responsibilities, its success was not always complete. In 1832, the Supreme Court held that several southern states, notably Georgia, were infringing on the rights and sovereignty of the Cherokee

Above: A romantic depiction of the Trail of Tears, painted in 1942 by Robert Lindneux

Indians living among them on their lands. Chief Justice John Marshall and the Court ruled that the Cherokees were an independent nation, no different from England or France. As such, the Cherokee Nation was not subject to the power of any state. Any issues or problems that arose concerning its needs were under the jurisdiction of the federal government.

This was a serious blow to the states involved, which coveted the Indian lands for development and were not terribly concerned about the personal or political rights of the Indians themselves. In this situation, the states had the sympathy of President Andrew Jackson, who was unwilling to support the Supreme Court's ruling with a show of force. The Court did not ask federal marshals to enforce its ruling, and the states were allowed to continue doing as they pleased, which proved devastating for the Cherokees. In 1838, they were stripped of their lands and forced to migrate westward to Oklahoma. Thousands died on this long and difficult journey, which became known as the Trail of Tears.

A 1937 newspaper cartoon takes a poke at President Roosevelt for trying to pack the Supreme Court.

Intense political need could also pose a threat to constitutional law. In 1937, President Franklin Roosevelt attempted to gain control of the Supreme Court by backing a bill that would have added six justices, for a new total of fifteen. Publicly, Roosevelt cited the fact that six of the existing justices were over the age of seventy; the additional justices, he argued, would be able to help the aging men with their workloads. However, the not-so-public rationale was that choosing six new justices all at once would give Roosevelt an unparalleled opportunity to appoint men who agreed with his positions. It was a less-than-subtle effort to pack the Supreme Court with supporters, and Roosevelt was strongly criticized for making such an overtly political move. Fortunately, the bill did not pass the Senate. No lasting harm was done, and the constitutional separation of powers remained intact.

During the early 1970s, the Constitution was tested again when President Richard Nixon participated in several illegal actions that came to be known as the Watergate scandal (after an apartment complex in Washington, D.C., where a burglary sanctioned by officials of Nixon's reelection committee took place at the Democratic National Committee offices). When it subsequently became clear that the authorization for this burglary ultimately led back to President Nixon, he resigned rather than face impeachment and possible expulsion from office.

Two other presidents, Andrew Johnson in 1868 and President Bill Clinton in 1998, actually were impeached by the House of Representatives. Since the

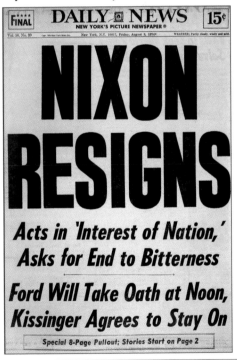

The Watergate scandal shook the nation and eventually caused the humiliating downfall of the nation's thirty-seventh president.

Senate acquitted both men, neither had to leave office. Overall, the impeachment procedure has been shown to be an effective tool in maintaining a balance of power among the three branches of government. It remains a clear reminder that no one is above the law, not even the president of the United States.

More recently, in the aftermath of the terrorist attacks on September 11, 2001, critics have maintained that the practices initiated under the administration of President George W. Bush threatened the constitutional rights of all Americans. Suspected terrorists have been held without regard for habeas corpus. Others have been tortured—a violation of the Eighth Amendment, which protects an accused person from cruel and unusual punishments—or denied access to legal counsel. Rights to privacy have also been subject to abuse (through wiretapping and other electronic surveillance), pitting constitutional traditions against the immediate threat of attack from the nation's enemies.

THE CONSTITUTION AS MODEL

If, as the saying goes, imitation is the sincerest form of flattery, then the United States Constitution has been flattered a lot since its inception. In 1789, only four months after George Washington became president, the French Revolution began, bringing an end to the absolute power of the monarchy. The French Constitution of 1791 (the first of several French constitutions during the turbulent 1790s) followed the American model, establishing three branches of government (with the king as the head of the executive branch) and giving some citizens the right to vote.

More expansively, the U.S. Constitution inspired changes in South American countries, beginning with Venezuela, Argentina, and Chile in 1811. Interestingly, the official name of Venezuela became the United States of Venezuela and its constitution featured a bicameral legislature.

Spain followed in 1812 and Portugal in 1822. Both of their constitutions also included rules supporting a separation of powers. The Mexican Constitution of 1824 distinctly reflected an American influence. It too called for a bicameral legislature with a lower house, the Chamber of Deputies, representing the population proportionally and an upper house, the Senate, containing two senators for each Mexican state. The Mexican Constitution was one attraction for American pioneers who began moving to Texas (which was then part of Mexico) in the late 1820s. In 1835, when this constitution was repealed by a different Mexican government, angry American settlers rebelled against the Mexican authorities. Several months later, the victorious Texans achieved their independence, which paved the way for Texas to join the United States in 1846.

In 1848, revolutions swept through many European countries, toppling governments in France, Prussia, the Italian states, Denmark, Switzerland, and Poland, among others. New constitutions providing for bicameral legislatures and establishing basic human rights followed in their wake. A half century later, American colonial expansion in the Philippines and Panama saw the influence of the U.S. Constitution spread to those countries as well.

With the end of World War II, new forms of government were devised for the defeated totalitarian states of Germany and Japan. In Germany, the constitution emphasized basic rights such as freedom of religion and freedom of speech. In Japan, the constitution created a parliamentary-style government with an elected bicameral legislature and included a guarantee of equal rights for men and women. (Although the emperor formally remained the head of the country, his role became largely ceremonial.) In 1949, newly independent India (having broken away from British rule) adopted a constitution that promoted many rights that by then were considered universal but whose ancestry could be traced to the American model created more than 150 years earlier.

In recent years, constitutional changes in Central American, African, and Asian countries have continued to draw inspiration from the American example of 1787. Representative legislatures and a separation of powers have proven to be enduring tools for the creation of governments.

THE ENDURING SUCCESS OF THE

United States Constitution is a testament to both its solid structure and inherent flexibility. These may at first appear to be contradictory qualities, but in fact they are not. Just as steel-framed skyscrapers are designed to sway in strong winds, so the Constitution was written to withstand great political and social tempests while remaining firmly in place. The executive, legislative, and judicial branches have established a secure and responsive base for representative government, and at the same time, the provision for amendments allows for appropriate changes to be incorporated over time.

Still, the fact that the Constitution remains in force is remarkable. It was written at a time when traveling from Boston to New York took several days and Pittsburgh was part of the western frontier. Yet today, when information crosses the country in the blink of an eye and satellite cameras in orbit can read the date of a dime lying on the ground below, the Constitution continues to anchor the American government.

Sometimes, the Constitution has come under heated attack. Strong leaders and powerful factions have tried to twist its words or ignore it altogether when such actions suited their purposes. "Good intentions will always be pleaded for every assumption of authority," said Massachusetts senator Daniel Webster in 1837. "It is hardly too strong to say that the Constitution was made to guard the people against the dangers of good intentions. There are men in all ages who mean to govern well, but they mean to govern. They promise to be good masters, but they mean to be masters."

> *"Good intentions will always be pleaded for every assumption of authority. It is hardly too strong to say that the Constitution was made to guard the people against the dangers of good intentions."*
>
> *—Daniel Webster*

Through wars and depressions and natural disasters, the Constitution has provided the comfort of political continuity and remained the intellectual anchor of the country. It has served, as Supreme Court Justice Louis D. Brandeis wrote, "to protect Americans in their beliefs, their thoughts, their emotions and their sensations." Looking back, this document did not guarantee that thirteen former colonies would be able to successfully merge their individual hopes and ambitions into a larger whole. Without it, however, they were surely doomed to further struggles that would have threatened their political survival. In a time of peace, the new United States Constitution gave a struggling young country more than a fighting chance to survive.

The Constitution
of the United States

FROM THE U.S. NATIONAL ARCHIVES &
RECORDS ADMINISTRATION

Note: The following text is a transcription of the Constitution in its original form. The portions of the text that are in blue have since been amended or superseded. Please visit the website of the National Archives & Records Administration, www.archives.gov, to learn more.

We the People of the United States, in Order to form a more perfect Union, establish Justice, insure domestic Tranquility, provide for the common defence, promote the general Welfare, and secure the Blessings of Liberty to ourselves and our Posterity, do ordain and establish this Constitution for the United States of America.

ARTICLE. I.

SECTION. 1.

All legislative Powers herein granted shall be vested in a Congress of the United States, which shall consist of a Senate and House of Representatives.

SECTION. 2.

The House of Representatives shall be composed of Members chosen every second Year by the People of the several States, and the Electors in each State shall have the Qualifications requisite for Electors of the most numerous Branch of the State Legislature.

No Person shall be a Representative who shall not have attained to the Age of twenty five Years, and been seven Years a Citizen of the United States, and who shall not, when elected, be an Inhabitant of that State in which he shall be chosen.

Representatives and direct Taxes shall be apportioned among the several States which may be included within this Union, according to their respective Numbers, which shall be determined by adding to the whole Number of free Persons, including those bound to Service for a Term of Years, and excluding Indians not taxed, three fifths of all other Persons. The actual Enumeration shall be made within three Years after the first Meeting of the Congress of the United States, and within every subsequent Term of ten Years, in such Manner as they shall by Law direct. The Number of Representatives shall not exceed one for every thirty Thousand, but each State shall have at Least one Representative; and until such enumeration shall be made, the State of New Hampshire shall be entitled to chuse three, Massachusetts eight, Rhode-Island and Providence Plantations one, Connecticut five, New York six, New Jersey four, Pennsylvania eight, Delaware one, Maryland six, Virginia ten, North Carolina five, South Carolina five, and Georgia three.

When vacancies happen in the Representation from any State, the Executive Authority thereof shall issue Writs of Election to fill such Vacancies.

The House of Representatives shall chuse their Speaker and other Officers; and shall have the sole Power of Impeachment.

SECTION. 3.

The Senate of the United States shall be composed of two Senators from each State, chosen by the Legislature thereof for six Years; and each Senator shall have one Vote.

Immediately after they shall be assembled in Consequence of the first Election, they shall be divided as equally as may be into three Classes. The Seats of the Senators of the first Class shall be vacated at the Expiration of the second Year, of the second Class at the Expiration of the fourth Year, and of the third Class at the Expiration of the sixth Year, so that one third may be chosen every second Year; and if Vacancies happen by Resignation, or otherwise, during the Recess of the Legislature of any State, the Executive thereof may make temporary Appointments until the next Meeting of the Legislature, which shall then fill such Vacancies.

No Person shall be a Senator who shall not have attained to the Age of thirty Years, and been nine Years a Citizen of the United States, and who shall not, when elected, be an Inhabitant of that State for which he shall be chosen.

The Vice President of the United States shall be President of the Senate, but shall have no Vote, unless they be equally divided.

The Senate shall chuse their other Officers, and also a President pro tempore, in the Absence of the Vice President, or when he shall exercise the Office of President of the United States.

The Senate shall have the sole Power to try all Impeachments. When sitting for that Purpose, they shall be on Oath or Affirmation. When the President of the United States is tried, the Chief Justice shall preside: And no Person shall be convicted without the Concurrence of two thirds of the Members present.

Judgment in Cases of Impeachment shall not extend further than to removal from Office, and disqualification to hold and enjoy any Office of honor, Trust or Profit under the United States: but the Party convicted shall nevertheless be liable and subject to Indictment, Trial, Judgment and Punishment, according to Law.

SECTION. 4.

The Times, Places and Manner of holding Elections for Senators and Representatives, shall be prescribed in each State by the Legislature thereof; but the Congress may at any time by Law make or alter such Regulations, except as to the Places of chusing Senators.

The Congress shall assemble at least once in every Year, and such Meeting shall be on the first Monday in December, unless they shall by Law appoint a different Day.

SECTION. 5.

Each House shall be the Judge of the Elections, Returns and Qualifications of its own Members, and a Majority of each shall constitute a Quorum to do Business; but a smaller Number may adjourn from day to day, and may be authorized to compel the Attendance of absent Members, in such Manner, and under such Penalties as each House may provide.

Each House may determine the Rules of its Proceedings, punish its Members for disorderly Behaviour, and, with the Concurrence of two thirds, expel a Member.

Each House shall keep a Journal of its Proceedings, and from time to time publish the same, excepting such Parts as may in their Judgment require Secrecy; and the Yeas and Nays of the Members of either House on any question shall, at the Desire of one fifth of those Present, be entered on the Journal.

Neither House, during the Session of Congress, shall, without the Consent of the other, adjourn for more than three days, nor to any other Place than that in which the two Houses shall be sitting.

SECTION. 6.

The Senators and Representatives shall receive a Compensation for their Services, to be ascertained by Law, and paid out of the Treasury of the United States. They shall in all Cases, except Treason, Felony and Breach of the Peace, be privileged from Arrest during their Attendance at the Session of their respective Houses, and in going to and returning from the same; and for any Speech or Debate in either House, they shall not be questioned in any other Place.

No Senator or Representative shall, during the Time for which he was elected, be appointed to any civil Office under the Authority of the United States, which shall have been created, or the Emoluments whereof shall have been encreased during such time; and no Person holding any Office under the United States, shall be a Member of either House during his Continuance in Office.

SECTION. 7.

All Bills for raising Revenue shall originate in the House of Representatives; but the Senate may propose or concur with Amendments as on other Bills.

Every Bill which shall have passed the House of Representatives and the Senate, shall, before it become a Law, be presented to the President of the United States: If he approve he shall sign it, but if not he shall return it, with his Objections to that House in which it shall have originated, who shall enter the Objections at large on their Journal, and proceed to reconsider it. If after such Reconsideration two thirds of that House shall agree to pass the Bill, it shall be sent, together with the Objections, to the other House, by which it shall likewise be reconsidered, and if approved by two thirds of that House, it shall become a Law. But in all such Cases the Votes of both Houses shall be determined by yeas and Nays, and the Names of the Persons voting for and against the Bill shall be entered on the Journal of each House respectively. If any Bill shall not be returned by the President within ten Days (Sundays excepted) after it shall have been presented to him, the Same shall be a Law, in like Manner as if he had signed it, unless the Congress by their Adjournment prevent its Return, in which Case it shall not be a Law.

Every Order, Resolution, or Vote to which the Concurrence of the Senate and House of Representatives may be necessary (except on a question of Adjournment) shall be presented to the President of the United States; and before the Same shall take Effect, shall be approved by him, or being disapproved by him, shall be repassed by two thirds of the Senate and House of Representatives, according to the Rules and Limitations prescribed in the Case of a Bill.

SECTION. 8.

The Congress shall have Power To lay and collect Taxes, Duties, Imposts and Excises, to pay the Debts and provide for the common Defence and general Welfare of the United States; but all Duties, Imposts and Excises shall be uniform throughout the United States;

To borrow Money on the credit of the United States;

To regulate Commerce with foreign Nations, and among the several States, and with the Indian Tribes;

To establish an uniform Rule of Naturalization, and uniform Laws on the subject of Bankruptcies throughout the United States;

To coin Money, regulate the Value thereof, and of foreign Coin, and fix the Standard of Weights and Measures;

To provide for the Punishment of counterfeiting the Securities and current Coin of the United States;

To establish Post Offices and post Roads;

To promote the Progress of Science and useful Arts, by securing for limited Times to Authors and Inventors the exclusive Right to their respective Writings and Discoveries;

To constitute Tribunals inferior to the supreme Court;

To define and punish Piracies and Felonies committed on the high Seas, and Offences against the Law of Nations;

To declare War, grant Letters of Marque and Reprisal, and make Rules concerning Captures on Land and Water;

To raise and support Armies, but no Appropriation of Money to that Use shall be for a longer Term than two Years;

To provide and maintain a Navy;

To make Rules for the Government and Regulation of the land and naval Forces;

To provide for calling forth the Militia to execute the Laws of the Union, suppress Insurrections and repel Invasions;

To provide for organizing, arming, and disciplining, the Militia, and for governing such Part of them as may be employed in the Service of the United States, reserving to the States respectively, the Appointment of the Officers, and the Authority of training the Militia according to the discipline prescribed by Congress;

To exercise exclusive Legislation in all Cases whatsoever, over such District (not exceeding ten Miles square) as may, by Cession of particular States, and the Acceptance of Congress, become the Seat of the Government of the United States, and to exercise like Authority over all Places purchased by the Consent of the Legislature of the State in which the Same shall be, for the Erection of Forts, Magazines, Arsenals, dock-Yards, and other needful Buildings;--And

To make all Laws which shall be necessary and proper for carrying into Execution the foregoing Powers, and all other Powers vested by this Constitution in the Government of the United States, or in any Department or Officer thereof.

SECTION. 9.

The Migration or Importation of such Persons as any of the States now existing shall think proper to admit, shall not be prohibited by the Congress prior to the Year one thousand eight hundred and eight, but a Tax or duty may be imposed on such Importation, not exceeding ten dollars for each Person.

The Privilege of the Writ of Habeas Corpus shall not be suspended, unless when in Cases of Rebellion or Invasion the public Safety may require it.

No Bill of Attainder or ex post facto Law shall be passed.

No Capitation, or other direct, Tax shall be laid, unless in Proportion to the Census or enumeration herein before directed to be taken.

No Tax or Duty shall be laid on Articles exported from any State.

No Preference shall be given by any Regulation of Commerce or Revenue to the Ports of one State over those of another; nor shall Vessels bound to, or from, one State, be obliged to enter, clear, or pay Duties in another.

No Money shall be drawn from the Treasury, but in Consequence of Appropriations made by Law; and a regular Statement and Account of the Receipts and Expenditures of all public Money shall be published from time to time.

No Title of Nobility shall be granted by the United States: And no Person holding any Office of Profit or Trust under them, shall, without the Consent of the Congress, accept of any present, Emolument, Office, or Title, of any kind whatever, from any King, Prince, or foreign State.

SECTION. 10.

No State shall enter into any Treaty, Alliance, or Confederation; grant Letters of Marque and Reprisal; coin Money; emit Bills of Credit; make any Thing but gold and silver Coin a Tender in Payment of Debts; pass any Bill of Attainder, ex post facto Law, or Law impairing the Obligation of Contracts, or grant any Title of Nobility.

No State shall, without the Consent of the Congress, lay any Imposts or Duties on Imports or Exports, except what may be absolutely necessary for executing it's inspection Laws: and the net Produce of all Duties and Imposts, laid by any State on Imports or Exports, shall be for the Use of the Treasury of the United States; and all such Laws shall be subject to the Revision and Controul of the Congress.

No State shall, without the Consent of Congress, lay any Duty of Tonnage, keep Troops, or Ships of War in time of Peace, enter into any Agreement or Compact with another State, or with a foreign Power, or engage in War, unless actually invaded, or in such imminent Danger as will not admit of delay.

ARTICLE. II.

SECTION. 1.

The executive Power shall be vested in a President of the United States of America. He shall hold his Office during the Term of four Years, and, together with the Vice President, chosen for the same Term, be elected, as follows:

Each State shall appoint, in such Manner as the Legislature thereof may direct, a Number of Electors, equal to the whole Number of Senators and Representatives to which the State may be entitled in the Congress: but no Senator or Representative, or Person holding an Office of Trust or Profit under the United States, shall be appointed an Elector.

The Electors shall meet in their respective States, and vote by Ballot for two Persons, of whom one at least shall not be an Inhabitant of the same State with themselves. And they shall make a List of all the Persons voted for, and of the Number of Votes for each; which List they shall sign and certify, and transmit sealed to the Seat of the Government of the United States, directed to the President of the Senate. The President of the Senate shall, in the Presence of the Senate and House of Representatives, open all the Certificates, and the Votes shall then be counted. The Person having the greatest Number of Votes shall be the President, if such Number be a Majority of the whole Number of Electors appointed; and if there be more than one who have such Majority, and have an equal Number of Votes, then the House of Representatives shall immediately chuse by Ballot one of them for President; and if no Person have a Majority, then from the five highest on the List the said House shall in like Manner chuse the President. But in chusing the

President, the Votes shall be taken by States, the Representation from each State having one Vote; A quorum for this purpose shall consist of a Member or Members from two thirds of the States, and a Majority of all the States shall be necessary to a Choice. In every Case, after the Choice of the President, the Person having the greatest Number of Votes of the Electors shall be the Vice President. But if there should remain two or more who have equal Votes, the Senate shall chuse from them by Ballot the Vice President.

The Congress may determine the Time of chusing the Electors, and the Day on which they shall give their Votes; which Day shall be the same throughout the United States.

No Person except a natural born Citizen, or a Citizen of the United States, at the time of the Adoption of this Constitution, shall be eligible to the Office of President; neither shall any Person be eligible to that Office who shall not have attained to the Age of thirty five Years, and been fourteen Years a Resident within the United States.

In Case of the Removal of the President from Office, or of his Death, Resignation, or Inability to discharge the Powers and Duties of the said Office, the Same shall devolve on the Vice President, and the Congress may by Law provide for the Case of Removal, Death, Resignation or Inability, both of the President and Vice President, declaring what Officer shall then act as President, and such Officer shall act accordingly, until the Disability be removed, or a President shall be elected.

The President shall, at stated Times, receive for his Services, a Compensation, which shall neither be increased nor diminished during the Period for which he shall have been elected, and he shall not receive within that Period any other Emolument from the United States, or any of them.

Before he enter on the Execution of his Office, he shall take the following Oath or Affirmation:—"I do solemnly swear (or affirm) that I will faithfully execute the Office of President of the United States, and will to the best of my Ability, preserve, protect and defend the Constitution of the United States."

SECTION. 2.

The President shall be Commander in Chief of the Army and Navy of the United States, and of the Militia of the several States, when called into the actual Service of the United States; he may require the Opinion, in writing, of the principal Officer in each of the executive Departments, upon any Subject relating to the Duties of their respective Offices, and he shall have Power to grant Reprieves and Pardons for Offences against the United States, except in Cases of Impeachment.

He shall have Power, by and with the Advice and Consent of the Senate, to make Treaties, provided two thirds of the Senators present concur; and he shall nominate, and by and with the Advice and Consent of the Senate, shall appoint Ambassadors, other public Ministers and Consuls, Judges of the supreme Court, and all other Officers of the United States, whose Appointments are not herein otherwise provided for, and which shall be established by Law: but the Congress may by Law vest the Appointment of such inferior Officers, as they think proper, in the President alone, in the Courts of Law, or in the Heads of Departments.

The President shall have Power to fill up all Vacancies that may happen during the Recess of the Senate, by granting Commissions which shall expire at the End of their next Session.

SECTION. 3.

He shall from time to time give to the Congress Information of the State of the Union, and recommend to their Consideration such Measures as he shall judge necessary and expedient; he may, on extraordinary Occasions, convene both Houses, or either of them, and in Case of Disagreement between them, with Respect to the Time of Adjournment, he may adjourn them to such Time as he shall think proper; he shall receive Ambassadors and other public Ministers; he shall take Care that the Laws be faithfully executed, and shall Commission all the Officers of the United States.

SECTION. 4.

The President, Vice President and all civil Officers of the United States, shall be removed from Office on Impeachment for, and Conviction of, Treason, Bribery, or other high Crimes and Misdemeanors.

ARTICLE III.

SECTION. 1.

The judicial Power of the United States shall be vested in one supreme Court, and in such inferior Courts as the Congress may from time to time ordain and establish. The Judges, both of the supreme and inferior Courts, shall hold their Offices during good Behaviour, and shall, at stated Times, receive for their Services a Compensation, which shall not be diminished during their Continuance in Office.

SECTION. 2.

The judicial Power shall extend to all Cases, in Law and Equity, arising under this Constitution, the Laws of the United States, and Treaties made, or which shall be made, under their Authority;—to all Cases affecting Ambassadors, other public Ministers and Consuls;—to all Cases of admiralty and maritime Jurisdiction;—to Controversies to which the United States shall be a Party;—to Controversies between two or more States;—between a State and Citizens of another State,—between Citizens of different States,—between Citizens of the same State claiming Lands under Grants of different States, and between a State, or the Citizens thereof, and foreign States, Citizens or Subjects.

In all Cases affecting Ambassadors, other public Ministers and Consuls, and those in which a State shall be Party, the supreme Court shall have original Jurisdiction. In all the other Cases before mentioned, the supreme Court shall have appellate Jurisdiction, both as to Law and Fact, with such Exceptions, and under such Regulations as the Congress shall make.

The Trial of all Crimes, except in Cases of Impeachment, shall be by Jury; and such Trial shall be held in the State where the said Crimes shall have been committed; but when not committed within any State, the Trial shall be at such Place or Places as the Congress may by Law have directed.

SECTION. 3.

Treason against the United States, shall consist only in levying War against them, or in adhering to their Enemies, giving them Aid and Comfort. No Person shall be convicted of Treason unless on the Testimony of two Witnesses to the same overt Act, or on Confession in open Court.

The Congress shall have Power to declare the Punishment of Treason, but no Attainder of Treason shall work Corruption of Blood, or Forfeiture except during the Life of the Person attainted.

ARTICLE. IV.

SECTION. 1.

Full Faith and Credit shall be given in each State to the public Acts, Records, and judicial Proceedings of every other State. And the Congress may by general Laws prescribe the Manner in which such Acts, Records and Proceedings shall be proved, and the Effect thereof.

The Citizens of each State shall be entitled to all Privileges and Immunities of Citizens in the several States.

A Person charged in any State with Treason, Felony, or other Crime, who shall flee from Justice, and be found in another State, shall on Demand of the executive Authority of the State from which he fled, be delivered up, to be removed to the State having Jurisdiction of the Crime.

No Person held to Service or Labour in one State, under the Laws thereof, escaping into another, shall, in Consequence of any Law or Regulation therein, be discharged from such Service or Labour, but shall be delivered up on Claim of the Party to whom such Service or Labour may be due.

SECTION. 3.

New States may be admitted by the Congress into this Union; but no new State shall be formed or erected within the Jurisdiction of any other State; nor any State be formed by the Junction of two or more States, or Parts of States, without the Consent of the Legislatures of the States concerned as well as of the Congress.

The Congress shall have Power to dispose of and make all needful Rules and Regulations respecting the Territory or other Property belonging to the United States; and nothing in this Constitution shall be so construed as to Prejudice any Claims of the United States, or of any particular State.

SECTION. 4.

The United States shall guarantee to every State in this Union a Republican Form of Government, and shall protect each of them against Invasion; and on Application of the Legislature, or of the Executive (when the Legislature cannot be convened), against domestic Violence.

ARTICLE. V.

The Congress, whenever two thirds of both Houses shall deem it necessary, shall propose Amendments to this Constitution, or, on the Application of the Legislatures of two thirds of the several States, shall call a Convention for proposing Amendments, which, in either Case, shall be valid to all Intents and Purposes, as Part of this Constitution, when ratified by the Legislatures of three fourths of the several States, or by Conventions in three fourths thereof, as the one or the other Mode of

Ratification may be proposed by the Congress; Provided that no Amendment which may be made prior to the Year One thousand eight hundred and eight shall in any Manner affect the first and fourth Clauses in the Ninth Section of the first Article; and that no State, without its Consent, shall be deprived of its equal Suffrage in the Senate.

ARTICLE. VI.

All Debts contracted and Engagements entered into, before the Adoption of this Constitution, shall be as valid against the United States under this Constitution, as under the Confederation.

This Constitution, and the Laws of the United States which shall be made in Pursuance thereof; and all Treaties made, or which shall be made, under the Authority of the United States, shall be the supreme Law of the Land; and the Judges in every State shall be bound thereby, any Thing in the Constitution or Laws of any State to the Contrary notwithstanding.

The Senators and Representatives before mentioned, and the Members of the several State Legislatures, and all executive and judicial Officers, both of the United States and of the several States, shall be bound by Oath or Affirmation, to support this Constitution; but no religious Test shall ever be required as a Qualification to any Office or public Trust under the United States.

ARTICLE. VII.

The Ratification of the Conventions of nine States, shall be sufficient for the Establishment of this Constitution between the States so ratifying the Same.

The Word, "the," being interlined between the seventh and eighth Lines of the first Page, the Word "Thirty" being partly written on an Erazure in the fifteenth Line of the first Page, The Words "is tried" being interlined between the thirty second and thirty third Lines of the first Page and the Word "the" being interlined between the forty third and forty fourth Lines of the second Page.

Attest William Jackson *Secretary*
done in Convention by the Unanimous Consent of the States present the Seventeenth Day of September in the Year of our Lord one thousand seven hundred and Eighty seven and of the Independance of the United States of America the Twelfth In witness whereof We have hereunto subscribed our Names,

G°. Washington
Presidt and deputy from Virginia

DELAWARE
Geo: Read
Gunning Bedford jun
John Dickinson
Richard Bassett
Jaco: Broom

MARYLAND
James McHenry
Dan of St Thos. Jenifer
Danl. Carroll

VIRGINIA
John Blair
James Madison Jr.

NORTH CAROLINA
Wm. Blount
Richd. Dobbs Spaight
Hu Williamson

SOUTH CAROLINA
J. Rutledge
Charles Cotesworth Pinckney
Charles Pinckney
Pierce Butler

GEORGIA
William Few
Abr Baldwin

NEW HAMPSHIRE
John Langdon
Nicholas Gilman

MASSACHUSETTS
Nathaniel Gorham
Rufus King

CONNECTICUT
Wm. Saml. Johnson
Roger Sherman

NEW YORK
Alexander Hamilton

NEW JERSEY
Wil: Livingston
David Brearley
Wm. Paterson
Jona: Dayton

PENNSYLVANIA
B Franklin
Thomas Mifflin
Robt. Morris
Geo. Clymer
Thos. FitzSimons
Jared Ingersoll
James Wilson
Gouv Morris

A Country in Doubt

p. 7, "If you ask the States . . .": Max Farrand, ed., *The Records of the Federal Convention of 1787* (New Haven, CT: Yale University Press, 1911), 1:433.

p. 7, "That great powers" and "The government . . .": Ibid., 1:430-431.

Chapter One: A "Firm League of Friendship"

p. 12, "This business, Sir . . .": Charles Francis Adams, *The Works of John Adams, Second President of the United States* (Boston: Little, Brown and Company, 1856), 3:70.

p. 14, "firm league of friendship. . .": Thames Ross Williamson, ed., *Readings in American History* (Boston: D. C. Heath and Company, 1922), 34.

p. 16, "Gentlemen, you will . . .": Octavius Pickering, *The Life of Timothy Pickering* (Boston: Little, Brown and Company, 1867), 1:431.

Chapter Two: The Constitution Takes Shape

p. 27, "When the legislative . . .": Contemporary Civilization Staff of Columbia College, *Introduction to Contemporary Civilization in the West* (New York: Columbia University Press, 1960), 1:1261.

p. 32, "When you assemble . . .": Walter Isaacson, *Benjamin Franklin* (New York: Simon and Schuster, 2005), 458.

p. 35, "There never was . . .": Gaillard Hunt, ed., *The Writings of James Madison*, vol. 2, *1783-1787* (New York: G. P. Putnam's Sons, 1901), 411.

Chapter Three: Becoming the United States

p. 38, "We the People . . .": Henry Hyde, presenter,

The Constitution of the United States (Washington, DC: U.S. Government Printing Office, 2000), 1.

p. 38, "in Order to form . . .": Ibid.

p. 39, "All legislative Powers . . .": Ibid.

p. 40, "by adding . . .": Ibid., 2.

p. 42, "Congress shall assemble . . .": Ibid., 3.

p. 42, "the public Safety . . .": Ibid., 5.

p. 44, "To promote the Progress . . .": Ibid.

p. 44, "Every Bill which . . .": Ibid., 4.

p. 45, "No Title of . . .": Ibid., 6.

p. 46, "President, Vice President . . .": Ibid., 8.

p. 47, "Advice and Consent . . .": Ibid., 7.

p. 48, "The judicial Power . . .": Ibid., 8.

p. 50, "in which a State . . .": Ibid.

p. 52, "The Congress, whenever . . .": Ibid., 9.

p. 54, "No State . . .": Ibid., 10.

p. 54, "the supreme Law of the Land . . .": Ibid.

p. 55, "All Debts contracted" and "no religious . . .": Ibid.

p. 56, "Ratification of the Conventions. . .": Ibid.

CHAPTER FOUR: A NEW ERA BEGINS

p. 60, "Our new Constitution . . .": John Bartlett, *Bartlett's Familiar Quotations*, 16th ed., edited by Justin Kaplan (Boston: Little, Brown and Company, 1992), 310.

p. 61, "cruel and unusual punishments . . .": Henry Hyde, presenter, *The Constitution of the United States* (Washington, DC: U.S. Government Printing Office, 2000), 14.

p. 61, "without due process of law . . .": Ibid.

p. 62, "If in the opinion . . .": Thomas Arkle Clark, ed., *Washington's Farewell Address* (New York: Charles Scribner's Sons, 1908), 13.

p. 65, "Equality of rights . . .": Henry Hyde, presenter, *The Constitution of the United States* (Washington, DC: U.S. Government Printing Office, 2000), 31.

CONCLUSION

p. 76, "Good intentions . . .": Edwin P. Whipple, *The Great
Speeches and Orations of Daniel Webster* (Boston: Little,
Brown and Company, 1889), 431.

p. 76, "to protect Americans . . .": Anthony Lewis, *Freedom for
the Thought We Hate: A Biography of the First Amendment*
(New York: Basic Books, 2007), 69.

FOR FURTHER INFORMATION

BOOKS

Amar, Akhil Reed. *America's Constitution: A Biography*. New
York: Random House, 2006.

Hakim, Joy. *A History of US*. Vol. 3, *From Colonies to Country
1735-1791*. New York: Oxford University Press, 2007.

Larson, Edward J., and Michael P. Winship. *The Constitutional
Convention: A Narrative History; From the Notes of James
Madison*. New York: Modern Library, 2005.

Maddex, Robert L. *The U.S. Constitution A to Z*. Washington,
DC: CQ Press, 2008.

WEBSITES

Constitution of the United States
www.archives.gov/exhibits/charters/constitution.html
  The U.S. Government Archives feature a close-up look
  at the Constitution and further description of the events
  surrounding its creation.

Constitution Facts
www.constitutionfacts.com
  This site provides a variety of information, games, and
  puzzles related to the U.S. Constitution and other
  American historical documents.

The James Madison Center

www.jmu.edu/madison

The James Madison Center for Liberty & Learning at James Madison University in Harrisonburg, Virginia, provides a wealth of material about James Madison from his papers and other sources.

SELECTED BIBLIOGRAPHY

Ellis, Joseph J. *American Creation: Triumphs and Tragedies at the Founding of the Republic.* New York: Alfred A. Knopf, 2007.

Hyde, Henry, presenter. *The Constitution of the United States.* Washington, DC: U.S. Government Printing Office, 2000.

Madison, James. *The Complete Madison: His Basic Writings.* Edited by Saul K. Padover. New York: Harper, 1953.

Mitchell, Broadus, and Louise Pearson Mitchell. *A Biography of the Constitution of the United States.* New York: Oxford University Press, 1964.

Rodell, Fred. *55 Men: The Story of the Constitution.* Harrisburg, PA: Stackpole Books, 1986.

Rossiter, Clinton. *Alexander Hamilton and the Constitution.* New York: Harcourt, Brace and World, 1964.

———. *1787: The Grand Convention.* New York: Macmillan Company, 1966.

INDEX

ABOUT THE AUTHOR

STEPHEN KRENSKY is the author of more than one hundred fiction and nonfiction books for children, including many about American history. He has written chapter-book biographies of Barack Obama, Benjamin Franklin, and George Washington as well as shorter works on the Salem witch trials, Paul Revere, John Adams, the California gold rush, George Washington Carver, Annie Oakley, and the Wright Brothers.